LORD, IS THIS RELATIONSHIP FOR ME?

Rosemary Godwin-Ese

DEDICATION

This book is dedicated to Jesus, my Lord and Saviour, who is always there for me and has been a significant source of strength in my broken seasons, when I had no one to confide in. He helped me push through each and every bad relationship. For this reason, I am thankful for where I am today. I also dedicate this book to the precious person reading it. I wrote this for the ladies. I believe this book will truly minister to you and help you endure the next stage of your life. I really want this book to speak directly to you and your situation, so you will be convinced that everything is working out for your good.

LORD, IS THIS RELATIONSHIP FOR ME?

Copyright © 2019 by Rosemary Godwin-Ese

All rights reserved. No portion of this book without permission may be reproduced, stored in a retrieval system, or transmitted in any form or by any means – electronic, photocopy, or recorded, without the prior consent of the author as it is strictly prohibited. Excerpts and links may be used, provided that full and clear credit is given to the author with specific direction to the original content.

If you would like to use material from the book for short quotations or occasional page copying for personal or group study, it is permitted and encouraged (other than for review purposes), prior written permission must be obtained on request by emailing the author on rosemarygodwinese@gmail.com. Thank you for your support of the author's rights.

Scriptures are taken from the New King James Version. Copyright © 1982 by Thomas Nelson, Inc. Used by permission. All rights reserved.

Printed in the United Kingdom

Published in the United Kingdom

ISBN Number: 978-1-9160600-6-7

My social media platforms:

- YouTube Channel: Imiebi Rose
- Blog: www.themodestlifebyrosemary.com
- Website: www.imiebirose.com
- Instagram: @imiebirose
- Twitter: @RosemaryGodwinE
- Facebook: Imiebi Rose

--- CONTENTS PAGE ---

INTRODUCTION: Lord, Is This Relationship for Me?	Page 1
Chapter 1: My History with Relationships	Page 8
Chapter 2: The Single Life	Page 32
Chapter 3: Celibacy	Page 41
Chapter 4: So, You Went Back to Your Vomit?	Page 47
Chapter 5: Christian Online Dating	Page 53
Chapter 6: The Correct Relationship Through the Holy Spirit	Page 62
Chapter 7: Wise Counsel	Page 68
Chapter 8: Prayer is Everything	Page 83
Chapter 9: Revelation	Page 89
Chapter 10: Sex for Marriage	Page 99
My Final Thoughts	Page 111

Introduction – Lord, Is This Relationship for Me?

Relationships are complex, right? Complicated? Difficult? Actually, I truly believe that the right relationship will have challenges, but a godly relationship will nurture authentically and at the right time. It will compliment you and be a blessing to you.

I am not saying that relationships are perfect, but God has one that is perfect for you. You will feel loved, and God will confirm it in your heart as long as you walk in wisdom, which means walking with God wholeheartedly.

Information online about godly relationships is becoming so popular nowadays, teaching us what and what not to do. We are in a generation now where there is so much information at our fingertips in comparison to our parents' days. I believe that this makes us more open to having dialogue about it, which is healthy.

I fell victim to romanticising other people's love stories, stupidly believing that there was some type of formula to be somewhat like theirs. But since we are unique people, our love stories will also be unique. I want you to be encouraged to allow God to write your love story; do not try to do it yourself.

I know in my heart that so many of you are in the wrong relationships. I unapologetically proclaim that those relationships need to and will be broken today in the Name of Jesus. I have been there so many times; however, when I re-dedicated my life to Christ, I decided to exercise obedience. It was a journey of stripping my 'own way' off, and at times, I failed and went back to my vomit. But there was a difference when I re-dedicated my life to Christ.

The difference was, I had a fear of the Almighty God, knowing that whatever I tried to hide from other people, He could see so clearly. *By fear, I mean reverence.* At that point, I knew that what I was indulging in was wrong, and I was not even trying to convince myself otherwise.

Relationships can either make or break you. Godly people pull you closer to what God has called you to do and are not afraid to correct you when you are wrong. Their true heart's intention is to bring the best out of you, pray for you, and stick closer than a brother (Proverbs 18:24).

On the other hand, a wrong relationship will derail you from the narrow path God has called you to (see Matthew 7:13-14). People like this will be abusive (whether emotionally, physically, sexually or psychologically) and will completely drain you.

I have observed poor relationships and have spoken to people who have been divorced (it's not easy!). God is amazing and can heal anyone who chooses to trust in Him, *but there are still consequences to our disobedience.* I believe that one of the most emotionally draining experiences is marrying the wrong person (someone else's husband/wife), and living with that for the rest of one's life.

Remember in the Bible when David escaped from Saul due to Jonathan's consistent warnings? Saul was trying to kill David due to his own jealousy and insecurities towards him as king. For an in-depth insight, read 1 Samuel 19. Two are surely better than one (Ecclesiastes 4:9-12). Saul ended up dying a foolish death because of his disobedience to God (see 1 Chronicles 10).

When people plan evil towards a child of God and anyone that is connected to you (be it family, friends or associates), I join my faith to yours that they will fall into their own evil plans. Be sure to intentionally intercede for people on a consistent basis. So shall it be that you will have spiritual prophetic eyes to see what is ahead.

We can see from the example of David and Saul that we need people to help us along this journey called *life in Christ*. We have to make sure that we are not doing relationships on our own and that both parties in the relationship have healthy accountability.

An example of wise counsel is found in the book of Ruth. Ruth felt a conviction to remain with Naomi, her mother-in-law, and continue life with her. Naomi was married before, but her husband had passed away. Her daughters-in-law Ruth and Orpah were also widowed (Book of Ruth chapters 1-4).

Ruth was open and willing to listen to the guidance of her mother-in-law when becoming the wife of Boaz. Under the guidance of Naomi, Ruth made herself visible so that Boaz would notice her.

This does not mean that you have to go out of your way to do the same, **unless instructed by God**. I truly believe that when you are walking with Christ and have fully surrendered to Him, you will be led by the spirit and be in the right place at the right time.

My prayer for you after reading this book is that chains will be broken in your life. If your family have a generational history of difficult relationships, divorce, sexual immorality or separation and may have passed down negative relationship advice, I pray that you will allow the Word of God to transform your mind, along with the help of this book. In order to maintain healing and transformation, it is vital that we walk in the ways of the Lord in **obedience**.

I also pray that if you are in an intimate relationship that God has not confirmed, and you are fully aware that He has sent warning signs, believe that God will grant a strong conviction, giving you the spiritual insight to see more clearly. Dreams and visions will outline the obvious for you to leave that relationship in the name of Jesus. If you can leave whilst we are still in the introduction part of this book, then HALLELUJAH!

My intention and heart's desire behind this book is to share my experiences about relationships, for you to be able to confidently know whether he is the one for you. May there be no confusion, in the name of Jesus.

A while back, I remember my Pastor at the time, saying something profound to me that will remain in my life: "Life is created for us to enjoy." Spending the **best years** of your life in the wrong relationship will cost a lot. Use your present journey to direct you into the life God wants you to have.

CHAPTER 1

MY HISTORY WITH RELATIONSHIPS

"Oh please, what do you know? Do you even have a boyfriend?"

I bumped into a mutual friend and decided to pick his brain about marriage. Although he had been married for a year at the point of discussion, I asked him what he could tell me about being married. He said, and I quote: ***"Marrying the right person gives you a prayer partner, but marrying the wrong person gives you a prayer point**. **The more you know about yourself, the easier it is to choose a life partner."***

This was such wisdom and confirmation of the truth flowing in my heart. Finally, the revelation of waiting for the right person dawned on me. It makes so much sense as to why I was confused years ago.

I was going through my season of the wilderness in my early to late teens. It was a bad time for me to get into relationships. I was so confused, unsure of my true identity, and in addition to that, I was dealing with family issues that caused so much damage. I lost my virginity at the age of 14 and had two main (what I thought were serious) relationships.

I was raised in London and have two brothers and two sisters. My parents came from Nigeria and worked hard so that we could have a better quality of life. I thank God for my parents. No family is perfect, but I would not change my family for anything, as it is where God placed me. I love them all dearly, and I thank God for their lives.

By the grace of God, I was raised as a Christian. I remember having a sweet relationship with God as a child. I would sing to Him alone in my room after reading my cute story Bible.

My mum and I attended a Church of England parish when I was a child, then we moved on to a Catholic Church, in my early teens and when I was age 23 (after re-dedicating my life back to the Lord), I started attending Hillsong. Now I am currently attending Mustard Seed Chapel International. Because of my foundation of growing up as a Christian, I always knew that God was real, even when I backslid and did my own thing.

I identify as a non-denominational Christian. This essentially means that I am someone who is not attached to any denomination, but is a student of the Bible for life and simply follows Jesus.

Family issues and seeking attention I could not get at home drove me to attend clubs and bars often at the young age of 14. I actually snuck out of the window to do this, because I obviously was not allowed to go to these places! I see how God covered me even when I put myself at a huge risk. Attention from males was my weakness.

The Holy Spirit dwells within me and has given me the strength to overcome this. I still get tempted like any other person, but God consistently keeps and enables me on the right path. He is with me, always.

In this book, I will mention four relationships. Two were with exes before I re-dedicated my life to Christ, and two were with people who came into my life thereafter. The first two exes that I will discuss are those I was with before I gave my life to Christ. The first ex we will call Jack. He is my ex fiancé. The second we will call Josiah. This was what I would describe as a rebound relationship.

A rebound relationship is someone you get with to try to run away from the fact that you have not healed from your previous relationship. This is detrimental, as it will never end well. Using another human being is never a good idea. We will discuss the other two relationships, post re-dedication to Christ, later.

Josiah was a white male. I had never been in an interracial relationship before this, and I received quite interesting reactions. I will not spend too much time on the topic, but let's just say that I got a lot of stares and, *"Oh, it's like that"* comments from friends.

Now that I know myself better, my preference is definitely a black man, but I am open-minded. God is NOT limited to race! We are all one in Christ. I was definitely ignorant back then in thinking that being with a white man may have produced a better experience. Because of the differences in our upbringing, I assumed overall that white men are more affectionate. But the truth is, humans are humans. Just make sure you get with the right one.

In no way am I bitter towards any of my exes and if any of them are reading right now, there are no hard feelings. Ladies, forgiveness is so important. If you are struggling with the impact of being mistreated by an ex, or anyone, for that matter, ask the good Lord to give you the strength, grace, and change of heart, in order to forgive.

My family in particular supported me in these two relationships. My exes actually came to my house on a few occasions and were welcomed. I appreciate that my parents may have expected me to marry either one of them, so they showed their support in that way.

I met Jack at the club, and we started to speak shortly after that. The friendship stage was fast forwarded into an intimate relationship. Eventually, he became my fiancé. I met him through another man at the club that accompanied me. I was not in a relationship with this man; we were more 'friends' than anything. I had this obsession with being friends with males that I was not in a relationship with.

I now see that because I was not close with my dad, I tried to fill in the gap with other males. This friend drove off with my jacket in the car. He was the 'jealous type,' especially when I spoke to other men at the club. My understanding is that he got fed up of seeing me socialising with other men, so he left.

I was shocked, and Jack observed it. He paid for a cab for me to get home. He said that I should let him know when I reached my destination. I was really thankful for his help. I was only 17. I was vulnerable and wanted to be with someone so much that I allowed anyone in my life without consulting God.

The truth is that he saw my vulnerabilities and used them to his advantage. Men are able to analyse a woman and measure up whether he will take her seriously or not. What did I know about the seriousness of what I was doing, anyway? Well, I knew something was not right, but the urge to feel wanted mattered more.

Of course, if I knew what I know now, I would not have done it. This makes me pose the question: What would it take for your standards to be compromised? An expensive gift, sweet talk, or someone that will spend months getting to know you, just to sleep with you?

I was so broken that I did not understand my own brokenness. Being in a relationship with someone about eight years older than me was the way forward, *so I thought*. The main issue within my household was that my parents had conflicting issues in their marriage and did not explain anything to me back then.

This led to my dad moving out; although he was able to see us from time to time and support financially. My parents tried playing 'happy family' and carried on as usual. I did not have much to say as I was confused and felt the need to go along with it. I was told not to tell anyone of the situation at home, so I felt forced to lie to those around me that all was well all in the name of 'it's no one's business.'

I always felt lied to, like something was wrong at home. This was because of the limited communication at the time. The situation made me feel uncomfortable and needy of attention from my fiancé. My fiancé was a Muslim.

He gave me a Quran, but it did not change my life the way Jesus did. I honestly did not read it much, but when I flicked through it, it did not speak to my soul or ignite my spirit the way that the Holy Bible did. I remember insisting that I would never become a Muslim.

The relationship with Jack was no good for me and eventually broke down. He used sex to control me and said it would be hard for me to find anyone like him, so I should just stay with him. I was very unwell physically. I went to the doctor often, but they were unable to diagnose me. I had random back pains and would often feel light-headed. I truly believed this was a spiritual issue.

It was like he wanted me to remain weak and vulnerable so he could control me. It felt so toxic, especially when he told me he was involved in witchcraft. My lack of experience did not allow me to connect the dots until I was 20. That was when I re-dedicated my life back to Christ initially and left the relationship.

I broke up with Jack when I realised he was cheating on me. He wanted me to think that our relationship was real, so he gave me a key to his place. However, I knew he was not being 100% with me. He used to let me use his laptop to do my university essays, so I became an investigator and snooped through his emails.

I monitored over a period of time that he was communicating with a woman that he wanted to marry, but I kept quiet until I built up enough evidence. I saw a particular email where he was talking about me. He said that I was "looking after him" and that I was "okay," but that she was the one he really wanted to marry. He told her how much he loved her and that he could not wait to marry her. It was heart-breaking to read.

He said a lot more. Some of it, I do not remember, and most of it is not worth repeating. I sent him an email, forwarding him his mail to her saying something along the lines of, "Since you want to cheat on me, this relationship is over." When he got home from work, I told him to check his emails later, because I had a surprise email for him. I then went home. He was quiet for two days. Then on the third day after I sent the email, he started phoning me non-stop.

I ignored all calls. The day after I broke up with him, I went to visit a male friend. His was another number that I kept in my phone *just in case*. I knew that he liked me. I just did not want to have any form of intimacy with him. I needed the company to run away from my pain. So I enjoyed the attention while it lasted.

About a week later, Jack turned up at my house asking me why I was ignoring him and torturing him. He ended up manipulating me, and in summary, we went back and forth in our relationship for a few weeks, trying to hold on to what was already dead, before I finally cut him off completely.

Thereafter, I got in touch with another one of my "male friends," and we entered a "friends with benefits" relationship. We had both experienced recent breakups, so we decided to vent to one another about it and book a hotel room to use one another for sex. This was really inappropriate! But the whole rebound thing is a real thing!

This is why you need to study someone that you want to get into a relationship with, to be aware of his motives, beliefs and character. Also, "friends with benefits" is a false concept that distorts the original meaning of friends and leaves both parties with soul ties.

The woman will most likely become emotionally attached. The man may take longer to develop emotions but can feel drawn back to the woman later on, possibly unable to articulate why, if he has not dealt with the soul tie.

A soul tie is what I understand to be a spiritual connection with someone. There are good and bad soul ties. The make up of the soul is the mind, emotions and will. The Bible is clear that Jonathan and David's soul were knitted together (1 Samuel 18:1). (Side note: this does not mean that the two men were homosexual; it simply means that they were God-ordained friends).

Negative soul ties do not come through sex only. They can come through emotions and conversations. This is why I do not entertain speaking to men at random that I have no business speaking to. As a Kingdom woman, my life has to make sense and be in line with the will of God. I pray over people that come into my life, asking God to reveal the reason.

I ask you to consider doing the same in order to avoid the many examples of where I went wrong in this book! So, if you find yourself struggling to move on from a relationship, you may have a soul tie. For more in-depth information and how to break this, I recommend a book by Dephne Madyara, **"Breaking Soul Ties,"** which can be found on Amazon.

When I left Jack completely, he started obsessively stalking me in the first few years post break up. He would not leave me alone. I was actually considering getting a restraining order against him. He would email, contact me on social media and turn up at my house.

Eight years after the breakup, he still continued being persistent, to which I ignored. Thankfully, after a few years, his contact with me was not at the same high intensity. There were moments that I responded and made it clear that I was not interested in him. I would block him when he discovered my social media platforms. I decided to pray, and God intervened.

The healing journey began for me when I was 21 years old. I got into another relationship with Josiah that I regretted because I had not fully healed yet from the previous relationship with Jack. In addition, I was still struggling with the spirit of lust. The devil tries to trick us with past weaknesses as a huge distraction to attack our anointing.

In the first few months of my new relationship with Josiah, I actually met up with Jack. This was when I was around age 22. I was completely honest with Josiah and let him know everything. Jack kept sending me long emails begging to talk, and I felt that *maybe* it was worth speaking to him one last time.

On that particular day, I had an experience that I would never forget. I was feeling really discouraged about meeting him again, and a group of Christians approached me outside the station where I was waiting, explaining that they were going around praying for people. They were really kind to me, saying that I was so beautiful and would one day make a good wife.

Only God knew how timely that was for me because I was wondering whether I would ever make it to marriage I did not tell them that I was meeting an ex when they asked for prayer requests. I let them pray a general prayer for me, and I kept my eyes open #trustissues.

When I met with Jack, he explained that his ex was into witchcraft and that was probably the reason that I was unwell when we were together. He explained to me that she would go out of her way to do anything to "eliminate" me from his life.

I was shocked that he would know that and not protect me, and I was fully convinced that he never really loved me. Their plans to get married fell through, and he realised that she was not genuine. He asked if we could try the relationship again. I said no. He even tried to use my faith to manipulate me, asking me to teach him about Jesus.

I felt sorry for him because he was experiencing multiple soul ties. This was evident because he called me the name of someone he was sexually involved with at that point in time, by mistake. He asked for a hug, and I declined. I walked away feeling that I had wasted my time.

I do not want you to think that in all of this that I was a saint. The saying that our relationships are a reflection of us is true! I had my own issues too. There was a time that I bumped into him on the train. He kept talking to me despite me ignoring him and telling him multiple times to leave me alone.

He said that he did not care that other people were looking at us and laughing at him for being rejected; he just wanted to talk. When we got off the train, I pushed him around and shouted at him. I was so frustrated and stressed. It is never right to hit anyone, but I felt that I had had enough.

He wrote me an email the next day stating how upset he was at my actions. I knew that he probably was sad about it, but I also knew it was the devil's attempt to manipulate me to get back with him. Although I was in a relationship with Josiah at the time, I felt guilt and upset at my actions.

In saying this, I have a flashback of a time in my relationship with Jack. I went through his phone and found out that he had gone on a date with another woman that evening! I confronted him and pushed him, shook him, and asked him why he was cheating on me and what I had done to deserve it.

I should have just left him. It was like I was begging him to just love me like how Christ loved the church. I expected him to be something that I did not seek God to receive. I did not even understand what real love was at that stage. I just knew that I did not like being cheated on!

He must have felt ashamed and sensed a blow to his ego after being pushed by a female. When I got home, he phoned me and threatened, "You're lucky I didn't hit you back. It would have been way worse than what you did to me." He was toxic, and so was I. We were toxic together and bad for each other.

My relationship with Josiah lasted for about two years. Looking back, I felt that the relationship was very forced, and I was not in a good place at the time. He actually asked if I could move in with him in the first few months of our relationship. He offered me his keys, and when I declined, it was like he despised me in secret, I later realised. Some people just get in relationships to have someone to share their mortgage payment, I have learnt!

We were in the relationship to seek "temporary company." I found a letter that Josiah wrote to his ex while we were together, and I felt cheated on. He was telling her that he missed her and how hurt he was that she cheated on him. Yes, emotional cheating is still form of cheating, ladies!

I went through his phone (when I had the chance, as he hid it from me always!) and saw that he was texting other women, like he was getting to know them on a deeper level. I felt so low, and I felt cheated on again! These actions, such as secrecy, are signs that a man is not ready to fully commit.

I remember Sunday 11th of August 2013, Josiah and I broke up after the Holy Spirit was tugging on my heart for months that the relationship was not right for me, but I would not listen. I felt I could not let go, because if I did, I would not have anyone else. Huge lie! I cried and asked him if I did anything wrong which caused the initial break up. I later realised that the breakup was the best thing he did for me.

I told Jesus, "Okay, Lord, I will follow you. I am ready," on the same day of the breakup. I now celebrate each year on 11th of August. In 2019, I turned six years old in the Lord. Ever since I re-dedicated my life back to Christ (for the second time), there has been a process of sanctification. It has not been perfect, but I have **changed**.

I was definitely one of those ladies who posted Jack and Josiah all over my social media. With Josiah especially, it seemed like it was an image thing, when people celebrated the fact that I was with a white man. One lady on my Facebook even commented, "You are going to have mixed babies!" – as if that was a marker of success! I even posted video diaries of Josiah on my YouTube channel.

I noticed that he never liked being on camera, nor did he wish to be on my channel. One of my viewers posted a comment on one of our videos (long deleted now!) and mentioned that it may not be a good thing that he does not want to show his face. She made me think and pose the question: *Why and what would he have to hide?*

In contrast, when I was in relationships post re-dedication to Christ, I did not post them on social media. As someone that is following the Lord and on a public platform, I felt indebted to always check my heart and make sure that I was not showing off, just to say, "I have a partner." I was not completely confident that these were my life partners, so it was not wise to start showing them off.

I fell into smoking weed before I was with Jack and Josiah, in my mid to late teens. Because of this habit, I attracted men that also did this. Smoking cannabis ended up being one of our main activities in our relationship.

So, you may understand why I felt that the relationships were never genuine. When you always feel the need to be in an intoxicated state of mind, running away from reality, how can you form a relationship that makes sense?

Quite simply, any substance that affects your sober state of mind indicates that there is something in your reality that you should start to deal with. It took me years to realise this – I spent so many years of running and living in denial, that I had to get to know myself after being sober again.

Years after I re-dedicated my life to Christ, I entered a short relationship. But God did not approve! I felt that after two and a half years of being single, I was tired and lonely. This was around 2016.

I was fed up of being single and needed comfort. I missed being hugged, receiving sweet and thoughtful text messages and feeling wanted by a man. We would hug, kiss and touch with clothes on but I did not go further than that. I am not proud of this behaviour (as I see it as sexual), but I stuck to my conviction of no penetrative sex.

I realised this relationship stemmed from the way that I felt in my relationship prior to that; I felt rejected and *still* had not fully healed! In this instance, I was still following Jesus and working on walking away from that relationship. The person that I was with at the time knew this, but he was still manipulative. I had to completely cut him off a few months later in order to safely move on with my life. I got busy with serving God and did not return back.

I learnt that setting healthy boundaries based on my human weaknesses was vital for my growth and strength for the road ahead, because I am the type of woman that will commit. It only makes sense to give my all to someone that God already confirms to me.

Our selfish nature always wants to have its way, and the desire to be in a relationship will not necessarily disappear. This is why it is a daily decision to choose Jesus and not our worthless sin.

We were created by God to be in pure relationships, so marriage will always be a desire for those that want to pursue it. There is nothing wrong with this, but make sure you flee away from sexual immorality, flirting and inappropriate relationships. This is something I highly advise you to practice before entering into a relationship. You do not want to get hurt like I did. As believers of Christ, we have to be intentional.

1 Corinthians 6:18 (NKJV) tells us that we should *"flee sexual immorality. Every sin that a man does is outside the body, but he who commits sexual immorality, sins against his own body."*

1 Timothy 5:1-2 (NKJV) says that we should *"not rebuke an older man, but exhort him as a father, younger men as brothers, older women as mothers, younger women as sisters, with all purity."*

According to 1 Timothy 5:1-2, we are all family, right? So, lusting after a brother that is not my husband is just not right. I do not know if you have ever thought about it like that, but we are called to *a life of purity*, so let us do all that we can to live right before the Lord.

If you are still struggling, continue to seek the Lord and have people around you that can hold you accountable. We were not created to do it alone, and you may be surprised at how many people struggle with this issue.

Trust and believe that when it is time for God to present your husband, no one will be able to shut the door! Learn to enjoy your single season. It is beautiful. Author Christina Tosin Fasoro wrote a book named **"The Singleton,"** which I know will be a blessing to you during your season of waiting.

CHAPTER 2

THE SINGLE LIFE

In my early Christian days, I tried practicing being single after the breakup with Jack. Being a 20-year-old, I was not fully mature in the Lord. Maturity would have come if I had sought it, but I was not completely dedicated. I would try to plan my own ways and say to myself that I had overcome the temptation to have sex.

My goal then was to seek a man that would abstain from sex as well. As long as his heart's intention was not solely sex, then it was not that important whether or not he was saved.

Looking back, I am so thankful that I did not marry those men that I once desired. God healed my physical and emotional well-being. However, I did not understand the spiritual side of relationships and the soul ties that were attached to them. I had promised to live a life of celibacy but did not fully commit to it until I reached the age of 23.

When I got into a relationship at the age of 21 with Josiah, I told him that I would like to wait until marriage to have sex. After four successful months of no sexual activity, I allowed him to convince me that participating in sexual activities would be a sacrifice that I was willing to handle.

I was foolish at the time as I had set no boundaries and had constant sleepovers at his house. Sometimes it is wise to keep your celibacy journey to yourself, whilst being conscious about setting appropriate boundaries. I think we ladies make the mistake of telling our personal business too early at times.

Men by nature are competitive. If you tell them too early, they may do all they can do to get you to have sex with them to prove something to their egos.

My lesson was learnt: A **_true man of God would not put me in a compromising situation but would respect my purity_**. The Bible teaches us in *Ephesians 5* that the husband is to wash his wife with the water of the Word.

If the man you are in a relationship with right now is not practicing this or is unwilling to start quickly practicing it, do not expect to see growth or a healthy relationship suddenly, prior to marriage.

Ephesians 5:25-26 (NKJV) says, "**Husbands, love your wives, just as Christ also loved the church and gave Himself for her that He might sanctify and cleanse her, with the washing of water by the word.**"

In my time of being single, I had time to think about my past relationships and understand my pain. I was operating from a place of insecurity and tried to convince myself that my ex could make me happy – poor him! I learnt that the emotion of happiness itself is a temporary emotion, but true joy is more consistent, and it comes from who I know (Jesus) and what I know about Him.

Happiness is also a choice that we have to choose to work on daily, for longevity. Since I decided to re-dedicate my life to Christ after the breakup, I conclusively made the decision that I would finally become obedient to His Word.

From then on, God gave me a plan, a purpose and granted me my dream job. He started me in ministry without me knowing it when He told me to lead a ministry called Pinky Promise in East London (a women's ministry coined by Heather Lindsey in Atlanta).

About six weeks after Josiah broke up with me, I started a master's degree in Criminology. The timing was perfect, as I was able to get myself together emotionally, after the initial shock and disappointment. I did not realise it then, but this was a great new start for me.

After being more intentional with self-care, I lost weight, started to see growth in my hair, and regained my confidence. I could not believe it: I was content in my life, wanting nothing but Jesus. The single life began for me.

It did start off lonely, but God kept me! It took two years to fully heal from the relationship with Josiah. I wanted to live a life of purity, and I am so thankful because my master's degree gave me hope that I would get my dream job as a Probation Officer, which is what I am currently working as now.

Spiritually, it has been the best season of my life. I do not have to worry about whether or not I will get my period on any given month because of sexual activity. I have saved myself a lot of energy against negative dealings and strains that come with a relationship that I am not supposed to be in.

There is a scripture that the Apostle Paul uses when he knows what is right but practically does not follow through:

Romans 7:15-20 (NKJV) says: *(15) "For what I am doing, I do not understand. For what I will to do, that I do not practice; but what I hate, that I do. (16) If, then, I do what I will not do, I agree with the law that it is good. (17) But now, it is no longer I who do it, but sin that dwells in me. (18) For I know that in me (that is, in my flesh) nothing good dwells; for to will is present with me, but how to perform what is good I do not find. (19) For the good that I will do, I do not do; but the evil I will not do, that I practice. (20) Now if I do what I will not do, it is no longer I who do it, but sin that dwells in me."*

I have not entertained penetrative sex for six years. As mentioned in chapter one, I did backslide around two years into my celibacy journey and kissed a man (in 2016) that I was not supposed to on a few occasions, letting his hands wander, because I felt *lonely*. I was tired of singleness and needed to be held, loved and wanted.

I went through a period of beating myself up inside about this, feeling like I had failed at the whole Christian walk. I had to really let God remind me that He forgives and forgets about my sin (Psalm 103:12). Do you find that we that hold onto things longer than we should? I later learnt to see that each new day is an opportunity to try again. So, I promised myself that I would do better.

It took a while for me to break free, dealing with guilt and shame of going back to my vomit. I did not have any accountability at the time. I am glad that I eventually broke free and stopped speaking to him.

What I realise is that, one already knows deep down whether a relationship is for them or not. Some call it a 'gut feeling' or 'women's intuition,' but I call it the **Holy Spirit convicting us**. **The more you know yourself, the better you can choose a life partner.**

Why is it difficult to admit that we get the whole relationship thing wrong at times? Be humble and willing to learn. We do not know it all.

I observe that some people start YouTube channels based on a relationship that has no future, just for attention. Next thing you know, the couple has gone their separate ways. Why does someone else's relationship seem so attractive? Well, God created us to be relational.

People see how much relationships matter and how much some members of the public want to drool over others, that it almost becomes a business! It seems that divorce rates are high among Christians. This could be due to the pressure that social media presents, especially when the comparison created through social media makes you feel that you should be married at a certain 'age.'

All these beautiful Instagram pages dedicated to stunning wedding outfits and parties seem to be getting to this generation. The truth really is that God has already written your love story. You just have to be patiently in position to allow it to play out.

My piece of advice is this: Just because others may have had negative relationship experiences does not mean that it will happen to you. The choices that you make daily (e.g. no sex, no pornography, a life sold out to Jesus) will determine your future. Build wisely and be consistent.

The Bible encourages us that two are better than one. God knows this because He said it, so be patient in waiting. Enjoy your life and seek the face of God about what He has called you to do! Being single is not bad. Yes, I have had my ups and downs, but overall, the journey has been worth it!

The next stage is a relationship leading to marriage, which is also a blessing!

Ecclesiastes 4:9-12 (NKJV) says, "Two are better than one, because they have a good reward for their labour (10) for if they fall, one will lift up his companion. But woe to him who is alone when he falls, for he has no one to help him up (11) Again, if two lie down together, they will keep warm; but how can one be warm alone? (12) though one may be overpowered by another, two can withstand him. And a threefold cord is not quickly broken."

CHAPTER 3

CELIBACY

I remember being told that being found by a man who will be willing to wait until marriage to have sex would be difficult. But I know in my heart that such a man exists for me. God created sex for marriage, and anything else is a lie. No matter how anyone will try to twist scripture, **marriage is the standard!**

1 Corinthians 7:9 (NKJV) says this: **"But if they cannot exercise self-control, let them marry. For it is better to marry than to burn with passion."**

It can be argued that the Bible supports polygamy. Some people would argue that by looking at the lives of David or Solomon, who had several wives, that having many women is a natural act. However, when wisdom is applied, you may agree that there is a difference between what Jesus allowed (instructions) and what man decided in his heart to do (documented scripture).

Once we understand the difference between the instructions that God gives us and the stories of those who came before us in the Bible, we will understand that living a life of sin willingly is not justifiable within any means. In addition, we are under a new covenant – one in which Jesus clearly outlined that marriage is to be between one woman and one man (Matthew 19:4-6).

Why does waiting until marriage to have sex appear to be a complex issue? As we know, the devil perverts everything, and this is one of the areas of his specialty. We were created to be with one person for life, but in tying ourselves along the way with other people, it makes it harder to move forward like we are supposed to.

When I decided to stop having sex and live a life of purity (no self-pleasure, etc.), I learnt that it would take time for my mind to renew and to see men as brothers instead of potential sex partners. I came to accept the reality that I am only going to marry **one** man, so being obedient by honouring God first with a life of celibacy will later benefit my husband.

I went to a singles' course in 2016, and the Pastor explained that the more premarital sex we have, the more we are building data on the 'memory card' of our brains. Memories of sex raise the chance of comparing our husbands to our previous sexual experiences, the Pastor said. This is not the way God created sex to be.

Yes, we can be "born again virgins," but **God cannot erase the consequences of our disobedience.**

Sex is a good thing. I see it as the bonding glue of marriage. The God that we serve is intentional. He gives us instructions for the betterment of our lives; not to take away our fun or make us confused. If you have experienced sex outside of marriage, you may well be familiar with the things that come with it.

Everything is spiritual, and if you find it difficult to get over an ex-partner, perhaps you should ask the Holy Spirit to guide you on how to encounter a spiritual breakthrough in this area.

Practicing celibacy when preparing to be found by your husband (Proverbs 18:22) will assist with clarity. If you notice your potential husband wanting to do **everything** to protect your purity until marriage, this is one good confirmation that he is from God.

This does not mean you will not be tempted, but you will hopefully both go out of your way to put boundaries in place to glorify God. Be discerning, though, as some men pretend to wait until marriage, whilst having sex with others.

It is better to build your own foundation on truth and the right thing, than to settle for less and compromise on your standards. I made up my mind that I was done with mediocre relationships! If you are easily influenced at this stage, it may be best to question whether you need a relationship now.

Being an indecisive person has consequences too, especially if you take your walk with Jesus seriously and do not want to create any sexual memories in your mind. It is a battlefield of the mind, but with time, you will get there.

Self-control is a fruit of the spirit *(Galatians 5:22-23)*, and waiting on the Lord brings great reward. We see in social media and the news from time to time how sexual immorality has turned our world upside down. When I read about sexual abuse cases and different forms of sexual immorality, my heart melts and cries out for mercy. I know that not every story is true; however, turning away from God and doing life on our own terms never goes well.

Celibacy was one of the best decisions I made. It helped me to recognise my worth, be in control of my emotions and have a healthier state of mind. With Jesus on my side, I could get to know someone without the complications of having premature sex. I used to feel something was being taken away from me spiritually and that I was not getting anything back in return.

"Why won't you marry me?" I said with tears in my eyes.

"Things are fine the way they are," he replied in anger. But nothing was fine as I heard his reply. It felt so cold.

I learnt that waiting on the Lord is one of the most beautiful experiences one can ever encounter. **Do not take it for granted.** You have to remember that He created us and knows the exact time, season and person! Get busy with what God has called you to do in your single season and do not be distracted by others who are getting engaged and married. Your time is coming!

If you are struggling with remaining celibate, the root issue is renewing your mind. You need to find a way study the word to learn the truth. ***Romans 12:2 (NKJV)*** says: **"And do not be conformed to this world, but be transformed by the renewing of your mind, that you may prove what is that good and acceptable and perfect will of God."**

Hebrews 12:4 (NKJV) says: **"You have not yet resisted to bloodshed, striving against sin."** How much do you hunger to serve the Lord and walk in His ways for your benefit? Some say that God is spoiling the fun or that it is a boring perspective to stay away from sex. But it is His Word that protects us and keeps our hearts away from those who would take advantage of us. He knows exactly what is best for us.

CHAPTER 4

SO, YOU WENT BACK TO YOUR VOMIT?

My journey of relationships is something that I struggled with in the past, until the last few years. Improvements were made as time went on, but it became a struggle because of the emotional baggage that I carried. It is no surprise that when I re-dedicated my life to Christ, it was a journey of real stripping, especially learning how to fully give my flaws to God and not deal with them on my own.

Romans 12:1 (NKJV) says: **"I beseech you therefore, brethren, by the mercies of God, that you present your bodies as a living sacrifice, holy, acceptable to God, which is your reasonable service."**

I have learnt that this does not just simply mean no sex. It is a heart posture. My love and hunger for Jesus must be above my vain wants. One of my favourite scriptures in the Bible is Isaiah 54:5, which says:

"For your Maker is your husband, the Lord Almighty is His Name, the Holy One of Israel is your Redeemer; He is called the God of all the earth."

When I started to see the Lord as my husband, my perspective changed. Yes, it really is deep! Being intentional in this area means that you must protect your purity at all costs. For example, I have placed boundaries in my heart as I am led by the Holy Spirit, being reminded that we are also called to deny ourselves.

Flirting was one of my weaknesses. There was a period that in every workplace, I entertained a flirtatious relationship. I thrived from the attention, so when the Lord convicted me, I knew I had to change.

What caused me to go back to something I promised God I would not do? We are living in a time when relying and responding to our emotions is something that is glamorised, but the Bible teaches us to leave sin behind and lean on the word of God.

Colossians 3:5 (NKJV) says, "Therefore put to death your members which are on the earth: fornication, uncleanness, passion, evil desire, and covetousness, which is idolatry."

Leaning on temporary emotions is what led me into the short relationship of comfort and pleasure in 2016. I have had never been single for such a long time, and I felt that it would never end. I made the mistake of entertaining flirtatious attitudes and an inappropriate relationship.

Instead of leaning on God, meditating on His word and setting up appropriate boundaries, I fell. The fact that I did not feel that I could speak to anyone at the time about this because of fear of being written off made it worse.

I felt guilty, but I maintained the relationship longer than I should have. If you have backslidden, do not feel that it is too late. The reality is that Jesus died for us while we were still sinners (Romans 5:8), and He loved us first (1 John 4:19) and still does! Please do not ever feel that you can be too far away from God to return. Gradually come out of your sin and see how far you will go with Him.

I know being obedient and staying celibate can take a long time, whilst being patient for the 'one,' but it is worth the tears and frustration in the long run.

Most people are living with their partner before marriage, especially in London, where living costs have increased drastically. It is more convenient to do it the worldly way because it is quick and easy. But there are long-term consequences that one should bear in mind. As mentioned earlier, using people never ends well.

Sis, if you cohabitate because you hope that it will lead to marriage, I am sorry, but you are only playing yourself. Statistics that I have come across over the years show that those that cohabitate and then get married have a higher chance of divorce. A study finds that premarital cohabitation is associated with lower odds of divorce in the first year of marriage, but increases the odds of divorce in all other years tested, and this finding held across decades (Institute for Family Studies, 2018). I encourage you to lean on the God who provides and pay for your own place. Keep your dignity and marry with integrity.

We should choose to be godly examples for those who are less experienced than us (Titus 2:3-5). I made a decision in my heart that I would do this for my children and generations to come. I believe that God wants to make a generational impact through us. He is looking for obedient saints to penetrate the much-needed truth that people are hungry for back into our broken society.

I urge you not to go back to your vomit. Delete and block his number and enjoy your life. I do not understand why people see blocking and deleting as something so rude and inhumane. I would rather get a toxic person out of my life than allow them to affect my wellbeing.

I would rather not go back and forth with, receiving and sending flirtatious texts to, or be at someone's beck and call when they are bored or want something. I just do not believe in making friends with people with whom I was not meant to make it past hello.

You are not being forced to stay in touch with someone, so just let it go! You will find that in your attempts to be pleasant and nice to your ex, you risk going back to your vomit. Just move on and entertain godly friends in your life.

Remember, every relationship in life either comes from God or the enemy. So, learn to pray over anyone that comes your way and ask God to show you the purpose of them being in your life. Relationships are one of the biggest downfalls for a Christian if one is not prayerful and careful.

CHAPTER 5

CHRISTIAN ONLINE DATING

1 Corinthians 10:23 (NKJV) says, "**All things are lawful for me, but not all things are helpful; all things are lawful for me, but not all things edify.**"

We live in a technological generation, which has made communication and working easier. Food shopping straight to your door, next day delivery and online dating! You can look online for your husband ... how about that? Wait – even better – *Christian* online dating!

In 2017, I felt that it was fine to put myself out in public for a date. After practicing singleness and celibacy for three years, I felt I was ready. I received a prophesy that I would meet my husband in 2017, but I am still single today. Actually, I think that I have received that prophesy every year since I have been single! There are many people in the body of Christ who are well-intentioned when they prophesy, but not every prophecy is straight from the mouth of God.

Many people talk about what they think based on temporary feelings, but being able to hear a word in season from the Lord is vital. At the time, I felt that I had to do something different! I tried Christian online dating, and it did not work for me.

I observed many people online who were not Christians. Some of my church members also engaged with online dating, and I wondered why they could not just approach some of the women at church instead? I also observed men that only wanted a Visa to the UK, and still others were just online for fun.

In the first week, I eagerly wanted to sign out and delete my profile. I was not comfortable with the messages I was receiving. I was tired of people getting excited over my looks, but when it came to the real deal, they were fickle. All I really wanted was just one man I could get to know. Scrolling and filtering through profiles and messages felt like I was shopping for the ideal man. Why did I decide to participate in Christian online dating in the first place?

I started Christian online dating because a colleague encouraged me to do so at the time. I listened and took the wrong advice, but now I realise that the person was uncomfortable with my standards of waiting because she had met her husband online and it worked for her. I explained to her that I was waiting on the Lord for my husband, but was she and others constantly challenged me regarding what exactly I was waiting for.

Seeing that other Christians were indulging in it, I felt in my heart that it was good to give it a go. I formed the argument in my head that over the years, I had met many people online through ministries. And since I have a business and found my church online, I figured I may as well make myself available online for my husband too!

Another friend informed me that he had a busy lifestyle and wanted to try online dating, but it did not work out for him. There is something about *1 Corinthians 10:23* that speaks to me regarding this. Just because you can, does not mean you should.

I was constantly being mocked during our lunch break by my ex-work colleague for my Christian perspective. I replied appropriately, sometimes defending myself and laughing it off. Through it all, I realised that she did not have my best interests at heart.

When I understood that my work colleague's heart towards me was not pure, I quickly stuck to my **original convictions,** and I urge you to do the same. God gives instructions to us and teaches us how to stay close to Him. He will teach you what your season is really about with no confusion.

The devil sees your desperation to be married too! This is why he will use people closest to humiliate and make you feel small. Remember, the devil comes to kill, steal and destroy (John 10:10). From this, I have learnt to be careful with whom I open up. I do not discuss my single life with people all the time, and I can now discern who I should relate with.

Some people make unnecessary comments or give unsolicited tips as to why I am still single, but it is not their concern. God is in charge of that! Seriously, singleness is not a disease.

I am mindful not to over share my experiences on social platforms because everyone is entitled to their own opinion, and I do not have the time or energy to argue with anyone else.

I am glad that I did not tell people to date online at the time that I was testing it, as I did not want to confuse anyone that is not strong in the faith. I didn't want to lead others to assume that online dating is the only way to be found, because I was still on the journey myself.

I was not sure certain people I knew would be disciplined or mature enough to pray consistently, as I know waiting on the Lord can be hard. I felt led by God at the time when I originally tried online dating, but when I look back, I believe it was my emotions that led me online. On the flip side, this has enabled me to now use my experiences to encourage others.

I met one man from the Christian dating website I joined. I was very disappointed after spending four weeks getting to know him. He looked completely different from his picture. The whole connection between us was off. Do you know what he told me? He said he had met several women who gave him a look of disappointment.

I had to tell him the truth and explained that he needed to take recent pictures of himself to give a true reflection his appearance. I believe he uploaded pictures of himself when he was a few years younger. He was a decent man, but I did not find a physical connection.

Another downfall about online dating is the realisation that there are a lot of women in one place online, and that the man you may be speaking to has access to these women at his fingertips. While you as a female may decide to speak to one man (if you make that decision), he is more likely to speak to multiple women, due to his hunting nature.

There are so many options online, all in one place. I know it is common for a man to speak to multiple women at the same time, before officially picking one. I am not saying that a man cannot partake in this activity. Some women also do it. However, 1 Corinthians 10:23 says:

"Everything is permissible, but not everything is beneficial. Everything is permissible, but not everything is constructive."

I wanted to be with someone who liked me for who I was, not someone who found it okay to indulge in speaking to a pool of women all at the same time. I could give him grace at the initial stage of getting to know me in the first few months (or less).

Speaking to multiple women for an extended period of time shows me that he is not into me, and I do not have time for that. How would I know if he was speaking to multiple women? The Holy Spirit would reveal it to me!

I also started talking to a man who was so excited about my looks that he proposed to me on the first phone call. He invited me to his house and had no shame about it. I was completely shocked! Then, when I challenged him, he blocked me quickly.

I remember telling a friend about it in order to get a male perspective. He told me that this man was likely being pressured by family members to get married as soon as possible. You will find all sorts online! And while I am not demonising online dating, you must be careful that you are led by the Holy Spirit.

Within 4-6 weeks on dating online, I decided that I was done with it for good. I was honest with myself that I got it wrong, so I shifted my focus back to the Lord and served Him while I waited on His best for me. Here I am today, still serving the good Lord. Online dating was not what I perceived it to be, which was disappointing for me at first.

I am not saying that God cannot use these kinds of platforms for His glory, because He is not limited in the way our human understanding is. How many people are willing to hear from God and act on His instruction? If God told you that He needs you to be single for another five years to complete an assignment, would you answer the call?

Being in a relationship is not the problem, but being in the right one is what counts. If I wanted to be disobedient, I could choose to live the lustful life and go back to my old ways. I had to get to a place of complete surrender to the Lord, knowing that there is a bigger plan. In addition, people are watching, and for this reason, I must live a life of integrity. Your life is a book, and people will read it. In other words, you are your own brand, and people are watching attentively. Be on your guard.

CHAPTER 6

THE CORRECT RELATIONSHIP THROUGH THE HOLY SPIRIT

Have you ever been in a situation where you thought trusting the Lord in your relationships was easy, but realised that it was not what you had in mind? How about when a random man tells you that he is supposed to be your husband? How will you know if a relationship is from God Himself if you struggle with hearing from the Holy Spirit? How is it that God has not given you the same revelation that He gave the other person?

I have been in two courting relationships in my six years of living for Christ. Let's call ex number one Jason and ex number two Kwame. In the years of 2017 and 2018, I experienced one of the most disappointing relationships ever. If I had known how it would have turned out beforehand, I would have made a run for it!
Nonetheless, I am glad, because it strengthened my faith. I met Jason, who I thought was ideal for me. A friend introduced us for the purpose of creating a website for my business. I made a few mistakes. I did not apply wisdom, nor did I seek clarity from God.

I did not guard my heart or maintain healthy boundaries in order to find out the real reason why this individual came into my life. Because of this mistake, the website did not even get developed.

Jason and I quickly went from talking business to talking about life, our experiences and what we desired in a relationship. Looking back, I have learnt that it is important that one should be very prayerful and careful about who enters their life.

I was not sensitive to the fact that the enemy uses anyone regardless of their original intention. If clear boundaries are not set, the enemy will deceive and manipulate.

I opened up to Jason about being celibate and moving away from worldly men that wanted a casual relationship. In my excitement that a Christian man had finally noticed me, I shared way too much too soon. I had noticed a few initial red flags that God warned me about, such as inconsistencies with his story.

He lied to me about something and confessed the truth a few days later. This was the perfect time for me to walk away, but I did not. I also noticed that he spoke about sex any chance that he could, using the argument that Christians tend to shy away from doing this when preparing for marriage.

At one point, we got closer than we should have because I allowed him to touch me (upper body, laugh out loud). After one other occasion, I made sure that came to an end.

Another red flag was his fixation with convincing me that I was his wife. I now see that it was simply manipulation. I remember hearing such stories before, where women have heard men say that they are meant to be! To be honest, I was quite convinced and felt it was serious. It *felt* real, but it was *not* real.

After four months, Jason's true colours began to show. We were out one day, and I had an issue with him remembering to charge his phone. This affected our communication, as he used to complain when my phone battery was low too.

I was frustrated because I felt that he was not listening to me, as I had told him to keep his phone charged so that it would not interrupt our time. We were out, and I made a smart comment towards him when he asked to use my portable charger, saying, "Do I look like a charging bank to you?". Laugh out loud – I know, I have sass! But his reaction showed me his true colours.

We had an argument, and he kept walking away from me, several steps ahead. His body language was fully telling me what he really thought! I do not know about you, but I find that really disrespectful and symbolic that the person is basically leaving you behind, all because you had a disagreement.

It was also in public – we were in a shopping mall! I should have gone home and ended the relationship. It clearly was not working. However, I kept the relationship going all because *he said* that I was his wife.

Shortly after that, we entered a long-distance relationship, as he had to work abroad for various reasons. We went from calling and communicating daily to barely speaking each week. I was confused – but we know that God is not in confusion **(1 Corinthians 14:33)**.

As soon as he left the country, I felt single. However, I was still inexperienced in the area of relationships in regards to really taking time, listening prayerfully to the Holy Spirit and waiting for a response. Whilst in London, Jason had promised to pray and do Bible studies with me daily, but as soon as he travelled, when I asked when we would start, he would make excuses or ignore me! The devil tried to mock my desires.

Even though I had been celibate for some time and was following the Lord, I still struggled with rushing into relationships like I did when I was in the world. I had many red flags and dreams warning me about Jason, but I still held on because I put the word of a man above what the Lord was showing me.

I am thankful for my prayer partner Doreen (love you loads, sis!!) and my Pastor at the time, who helped me tremendously when I needed it the most. My Pastor told me that the relationship was dead and I need to move on. I was spiritually exhausting myself praying for him, communicating with him and getting upset about the whole situation.

This is a classic example of how the enemy makes a fool out of God's anointed, and how at times, we women fail to measure up a man's words with his actions. In all of this, our relationship was very short. I should have ended it at the four-month mark, but I spent five extra months trying to make it work.

I truly learnt not to be led by my own emotions, purely because I 'like' or am attracted to a man. I have learnt not to take action until God reveals to me that I should. I now focus on the facts over my feelings.

CHAPTER 7

WISE COUNSEL

I have needed a lot of wise, godly counsel over the years. I have depended on experienced counsellors who were in healthy marriages and who have spiritual authority, particularly those who walk with the Lord and personally know me. It is important that we do life together as Christians and discern when speaking to the right people. The Bible is fully in support of wise counsel. **Proverbs 12:15 (NKJV)** says: **"The way of a fool is right in his own eyes, but he who heeds counsel is wise."**

I see many points in my past relationships that, had I taken time, been prayerful and told trusted friends every step of the way, I could have prevented wasting time. As a Christian, I believe that it is important to be mindful of building relationships too soon. Learn to be friends and gradually build gracefully together.

One of the things that I have highlighted in this book is being sensitive to the Holy Spirit and praying often about who to let into my life.

As I was going through the difficulties of relationships, God connected me with Doreen, who became my prayer partner. I felt led to open up to her. Months prior to that, I admired her beauty. I always say she is very beautiful both inside and out and that my spirit really connected with hers.

With people and situations, you do not always need to do a lot for God to reveal one's character. If your spirit finds peace and rest about someone, you will know it and authentically feel led to share your problems without being judged.

You would also want that person to stand with you in prayer. Doreen was very instrumental in my life and introduced me to her Pastor. She was so diligent in encouraging me every step of the way.

I had never experienced a friendship where one was so intentional about helping me out to such an extent. We know how we women can be with our emotions, when not being intentional about giving it *all* to God (yes, we are the weaker vessels), and at times, it can be seen that women can be envious or intimidated by one another.

Because of Christ, I am content in life. However, due to my contentment, it is not always received well. If someone is feeling the opposite way, they can tend to be envious of my peace and contentment. When I perceive this in certain scenarios, I try to keep my distance or encourage the individual as I feel led, remaining firm in my positioning in God.

I later learnt the concept of *destiny friends* – people that are in your life to help you reach your destiny, as Christ has ordained it to be. As we know, the enemy has his own destructive paths and will use anyone to steer you off course, as a Christian.

It is vital that you are aware of this too. I mentioned earlier the story of David, and how Saul wanted to kill him before his time. That story is such a great example of how God will send a friend like Jonathan to lift you up and intervene.

On the flipside, a negative friend would be a stumbling block, especially if you are unsure how to discern who to tell your secrets to. If they are envious, they can try to convince you that the wrong relationship is right for you. So be careful.

I have another prayer partner, Ope. He is a brother that is a positive example and offers sound advice on how a man of God should be. I did not have this growing up, so I take this as a blessing.

I believe as a woman, it is important to have genuine male friends. I realise that when the male-female friendship is from God, healthy boundaries fall naturally in place, and the friendship will be consistent. The flipside of this is when the enemy sends counterfeits to pose as a male friend, when really, they want a relationship with you. This has happened to me many times until I learnt the importance of discerning and having healthy boundaries.

It helped when I became aware of my inner and outer beauty and learnt how to tailor my kindness in such a way that would not encourage any inappropriate relationships. But of course, you can still attract a man when being extremely boundary-focused!

Ope also connected me with his Pastor. A good friend will always share good things with you. Prior to this, I knew his Pastor for quite some time and used to attend his Bible study years ago.

I used the opportunity to speak with him about my relationship when I attended their church event. He laid the foundation to help me see life from a different perspective. He encouraged me to remove myself from emotional decisions. I remember when we discussed the topic of a man telling a woman that he is her husband.

He gently warned me to make sure it was truly coming from the Lord, in my situation. He challenged me to ask God for clarity and to be expectant for a word.

After I spoke to both Pastors, I knew the relationship with Jason had to end. This just shows you the power of wise counsel! Being counselled gave me clarity and helped in my decision to leave the relationship.

I broke up with him via text message. He was barely speaking to me anyway, and I felt that his negligence spoke that he had left the relationship without really telling me, hence my casual approach! Prior to that, I had booked a flight to see him abroad, but I cancelled it shortly after. I got half my money back, but I was even willing to lose it *all*, as I had the conviction that I was doing the right thing.

Had I gone to see Jason, this man would have manipulated my emotions and used me for sex, because he was not serious about me! After years of working on my celibacy journey, I was intentional about not falling into sexual sin again because it is **not worth it**.

Please note, ladies: if you really want a successful marriage, do not fall into sexual sin. Yes, God can turn anything around, but for me, it is best to wait.

Since the break-up, it was clear that Jason did not *really* care, as evidenced by his empty promises. I realised that he was trying to see whether he could have sex with me, and when he saw that he could not, he lost interest.

When I messaged him that break up message, the response was that he would call after work. However, he did not call me for a few days. I made the decision to stop speaking to him completely. I have not spoken to him since we broke up! I took his poor response as further confirmation that future discussion would be a total waste of time.

I had actually expressed my concerns to him before the final break up about how I felt, stating that if he continued, I would break up with him. He manipulated me to stay, improved communication for a few days, then went back to his old ways. I had given too much of my energy and emotions and decided that enough was enough.

The advice I received was to ignore all messages and attempts to get in touch. I broke up with him in August 2018. He kept phoning me some days after before I blocked him. In May 2019, he tried sending me messages on social media, asking me to get in touch through his sister.

My relationship with Kwame only lasted for two months. I met him a few months after I broke up with Jason. He went to my church at the time, and I was so excited that I had finally met someone that I actually was attracted to! (it does not happen to me often!).

I got to know him through going on multiple dates in our short time together. He was a nice guy, but I started to notice subtle signs of emotional abuse. My feelings were not prioritised as I felt they should be. When reflecting on my ideal potential character of a future husband, I found him quite insensitive.

At one point during a phone call, when I asked him a Biblical question, I was once told, *"I did not phone you for a theology class, but I called to have a nice conversation."* Wait, what?

If any of you know me, you will know that I am very passionate about the Bible and food! I have other passions, like hard work, self-love and more. But I believe that those are my main ones.

So I loved speaking about the Holy Bible, but Kwame snapped on me! Long story short, he snapped a lot at me for being myself. We were not the best match, to be honest. Because of my negative experiences of being in unhealthy relationships, even as a Spirit-filled Christian, I did not catch certain things right away. My **emotions** blinded me.

I think that it can be very detrimental to rush into a relationship without giving yourself a chance to hear from God first. Getting to know someone on a friendly basis is one thing, but making some kind of relationship commitment too early is another.

Here, I made the mistake of getting with a man whose whole agenda was to rush into marriage because he felt pressured by friends and family. *Again*, I was seeking an answer from God whilst in the relationship instead of praying for that prior to entering it. This time, though, he did not tell me that I was his wife.

However, because he was rushing into marriage, when he felt that there was any interruption in getting to know me as soon as he could, he snapped!
One of the red flags in this short relationship for me, was when I would let him know that I was on my way home, he would not check that I got home safely until hours later, despite me texting him that I was home! We all have things that are important to us.

Call me dramatic if you want, but I know that a man that truly cares about you, would care about your safety and welfare. This can only be demonstrated in his actions! As my brother in Christ, Ope always showed me this example by dropping me off at home and making sure I was safe when we went out.

Kwame just had this stubbornness that meant he was unwilling to adapt. He said that he would leave his phone alone for hours and would only check it when he felt like it. I understood that he did not always want to be on his phone, but this was far too rigid for me! How can such preferences override my feelings and this relationship?

I was not asking for us to speak 24-7! Make sure you know who you are, your preferences and non-negotiables before getting into a relationship, so that you can see when someone is not for you. **No need to waste time** when you know what you want! Do not ignore red flags, no matter how little they may be! These things will only be magnified in marriage!

During this time, I was thankful for the wise counsel that I received. One of the major issues with Kwame was that he was not transparent. He wanted to hear my business but was very guarded when it came to his.

My Pastor at the time made it clear that in marriage, the two are one. Therefore, honesty is required, even when someone does not *feel* like talking about a particular thing. So I was surprised when Kwame was reluctant to tell me about his exes and why the relationships had ended!

He would open up but made me feel like he really did not want to. I personally think it is important to speak about exes because getting to know someone is your opportunity to study a person closely, to really know if they are God's best.

But when it came to me, and I told him my past, he used it against me, stating that he was concerned that the things I once did may come back. Wow, sis! It seems that the fact that God cleanses and sanctifies us was not clear to Kwame. But I do understand where he was coming from, given his trust issues in the past with women, that he shared with me.

At one point in our relationship, he did an online personality test and asked me to do it too and tell him my answer. When breaking up with me face to face, he revealed to me that he wanted us to take the personality test because he knew that us being in a relationship would not work.

That is all good and well, but I felt that I was strung along a few weeks after that, whilst he should have just broken up with me after the personality test. My friend told me I should understand that he probably found it hard to end it so soon and that he had to come to terms with it first.

I was thankful that God sent me a dream a night before he broke up with me. The dream did not make sense at first but I prayed and the Holy Spirit gave clarity. A few weeks prior to that, I observed clear signs that he was losing interest. I actually asked Kwame weeks before the breakup if anything had changed between us, but he lied, stating that nothing had changed.

The good thing is that when he broke up with me, I was already expecting it. I was upset because I had shared too much with him too soon. In that moment, I felt discouraged because I was wondering whether or not I would ever get married. But I was thankful to listen to wise counselors who reminded me of the facts and explained to me that Kwame wanted an 'easy time' of getting to know me as he just wanted to get married.

I was told by my Pastor at the time not to play into what he called 'psychological banter' of Kwame, who wanted to keep in touch with me or be 'friends.' As stated earlier, we have to be mindful of who we call a friend. He explained that he wanted to remain friends because he felt guilty for getting my hopes up only to break up with me.

I listened, did not respond to his follow-up text of checking on me to see how I was doing, as he struggled to do that in the relationship anyway! I blocked him shortly afterwards and moved on with my life.

When I saw him at church, I was thankful for friends that listened to me when I felt my emotions rising, because I was not yet over him. I was glad when he went back overseas, as he was in London temporarily for studies (he was considering settling here when he was with me, though).

Through prayer and God's divine connection with the people he placed in my life, I have been able to navigate my way through such situations. We need good examples in our lives, especially for those who did not get the opportunity (like myself) to have godly counsel by words and examples when growing up.

We should be able to open up to our loved ones and depend on God to do what He knows is best. I observe instances where people get into a relationship and refuse wise counsel due to the difficulty in waiting, and then they rush into marriage.

This is not healthy, and the enemy is serious about using this as a set up for disaster and heartache. Learn to discern trustworthy people. There are genuine people in this world. I am a living testimony that God used the people in my life to pull me out of the darkness I was in.

CHAPTER 8

PRAYER IS EVERYTHING

Having a relationship with Jesus has changed my life in every way. Such understanding of God and His purpose for mankind comes through reading and studying the word of God with the Holy Spirit as the main guide. This helps me to cultivate a healthy prayer life.

God has His way of communicating with His children. Personally, He used my close friends, visions and dreams to communicate and send warnings, as mentioned earlier. I would pray and receive dreams relating to my direct situation. Sometimes it can be confusing, as the enemy targets Christians by also sending dreams. Nonetheless, with experience, I learned to discern what God says to me.

The Bible highlights the importance of prayer. I incorporated this into my personal relationship with God and had real talks about what was on my heart, as I felt it was a way to heal internally.

Throughout the day, usually before I get out of bed and leave the house for work, I call upon the name of the Lord in prayer. I am inspired by the scripture that draws our attention to prayer. **1 Thessalonians 5:16-17 (NKJV)** says: **"Rejoice always, pray without ceasing, in everything give thanks; for this is the will of God in Christ Jesus for you."**

The importance of prayer is highlighted and how necessary it is in our daily walk of life. We should be in constant fellowship with God throughout our day. In all things, I developed a heart of gratitude in my season and thanked Him for everything, even when I was frustrated about my circumstances.

I told my prayer partner that I would write a book on failed relationships. I strongly felt many ladies would relate to the bad experiences I faced in past seasons. I know for a fact that I am not the only person who has been through heartbreak.

I learnt about myself in the failed relationships, which caused me to grow in the wisdom of the Lord. It pushed me deeply to study my Bible more and highlighted that I must surrender my ways for His ways and let Him know the state of my heart. Ultimately, I have learnt to desire that His will would be done.

One of the most important things I want you to take away from this book is the word *"authenticity."* Without an authentic relationship with the Lord, it will be difficult to know whether the relationship presented to you is from God or the enemy.

I use myself as a testimony because I know that even when I was making effort to develop my relationship with Jesus, I still failed with the men I had in my life. I did not apply wisdom in my relationships and decided to stay quiet, thinking such relationships will naturally go away, but it really did not end in the way that I expected.

I thank God that although the foundations with my previous relationships were unstable, He never let go of my hand and stood by my side even when I was unfaithful to Him, particularly with my inconsistencies of 'trying' to be celibate.

While I had weak moments, my boundaries were strengthened, and I used it as a way to reflect upon God's love and forgiveness. I decided that I would not entertain any form of sexual immorality, and committed to intentionally serve God with my heart, allowing Him to build up my character on how I could prepare for my future husband, in reference to Ephesians 5.

I believe that an unwise approach to prayer is speaking prematurely about a man that has not been confirmed to be your husband. How many of us have done that? I have! *Only when God informs you that a man is your husband is when you should move.* If He has not told you to proceed, please be still.

God should not be treated as someone you call *only* when you are in need. Regardless of how much you desire God to move on your behalf, if your prayers are coming from a place of emotions and frustration, God can tell. What truly matters is the level of faith and commitment you put into praying. Remember, without faith it is impossible to please Him (Hebrews 11:6).

Yes, I believe that my future husband will have flaws, as I already have my own. However, if he is really for me, we both should learn how to strengthen each other's weaknesses and not use them against one another.

We must learn to take the time and check our hearts to see how we can pour into our husbands, and vice versa. Focus on **your role**. If I do not take time to grow, understand and nurture my future husband, it will be hard to nurture, heal and develop myself as a woman. You need to have this mind-set before the stage of marriage.

> *Proverbs 24:3 (NKJV) Through wisdom a house is built, and by understanding it is established.*

Taking quality time in the Lord to pray and lean on Him is good for my mental and emotional state. I am at the stage in life where if I do not hear from God, I will not proceed in entertaining any intimate relationship. For this reason, I encourage you to pray without ceasing **in all things,** for this is a very good habit to have.

CHAPTER 9

REVELATION

The biggest revelation God showed me about some men is seeing how destructive they can be when a woman chooses to be vulnerable and open. I do not know why men do this, but feel they have the upper hand to use a woman's weakness for their advantage. I guess it is sin nature.

A man can tell you he loves you because you told him, but is that just a way to make you compromise on self-worth? A man can tell you he loves you, but will he stay with you? If a man cannot stay with you in minor mishaps and miscommunications, then do not waste your time.

I still had things to work on, including my personal development and relationship with God. It was not a good idea for me to enter a committed relationship if I did not feel complete in who I was at the time.

Looking back, Jason was emotionally abusive, and I too was rude to him because of it. I had to protect myself big time! *The funny thing about relationships is they are always sweet when they start out, but true relationships stand on the solid foundation of Christ when tested.*

I was distracted as I used to compare my story to other people on social media, feeding myself on false doctrine, which was not pleasing to God at all. At the time, I was naïve and didn't have a strong relationship with Him. I realise now that God grants wise counsel through His Word on all aspects of our lives. He wants us to operate at our highest potential!

Imagine if you made the decision to operate at your highest potential daily. What would that look like to you? I wanted my life to have meaning and pleasant reactions to help my followers and inspire them; however, I was not even getting the basics right.

In 2017, there seemed to be a trend where men and women made themselves available to meet a potential partner. **"You need to be in an environment where someone can approach you!"** social media would scream in my ears.

In today's society, Christian events are being promoted to encourage singles to meet and get to know the opposite sex. Bible scriptures, including the story of Ruth, are taken out of context.

Some men talk about the fact they need a woman like Ruth to approach them or give a sign to show interest. *I personally believe a real man goes after what he really wants.* Do not get me wrong: A woman should be approachable, but honestly speaking, men who are of God (and women alike) in this generation can be hard to find.

You can go out of your way and do what you like, but if you are so desperate for marriage, you will end up with the wrong person.

Social media has created strange dynamics for a man in regards to getting a woman's attention. This can be basic, effortless actions such as a man 'liking' a woman's picture on her social media account, and the woman at times being overly excited by it.

I am not saying that you cannot meet a potential mate on social media, but back in the day, men would approach women face-to-face and converse! Sis, it is only one like! I know that these types of men can slyly try to come back into your life gradually after so many years, making attempts to communicate with comments on your pictures and posts. But do not drop your standards for him, who could not keep you when he had you.

Sis, any man can check a woman's social media profile: viewing your story, liking pictures, leaving comments, sending private messages, etc.

However, how many can respectfully pursue you in Christ, take the time to know you over the phone, take you out, invest time, prayer and remain celibate with you, asking God to strengthen you? This generation of social media has made it easy for men to gain access to everybody. Do not be naïve and think that attempts on social media are sufficient. The truth is, that is too easy.

I will still stand on this: there are good men out there who know how to respect women not only on social media, but in person too. I know that it does not help that many women are out there showing a lot of skin on social media. It creates the illusion that this is all a man wants. With the rise of plastic surgery, it would seem that is the way to go for us, ladies, in order to not to be left behind.

But I realised that God made no mistakes when he created woman. A woman is way more than her body or outer beauty. A real man of God knows this, and yes, attraction matters, but most men prefer natural beauty. So do not follow all the social media hype or try to mirror what is commonly done out there.

Do not put your hopes on a man or your ex if he is simply showing interest in your social media platforms. Wait on the Lord, trust in Him, lean on Him, and He will provide your husband. DO NOT fall for these stupid distractions and lies. A wise person once said, when he contacts you, just IGNORE.

Abuse is playing a destructive role in the lives of many relationships in today's society. Men can often be spiteful and emotionally abuse a woman's vulnerabilities. Women can often take advantage of a man's kindness and patience, etc. It still all falls in the bracket of abuse.

I actually have a list of qualities written down that I would like to see in my husband. I remember sharing this with my my ex, Kwame. He made it seem like it was too much! In addition to this, abuse can also be seen as someone making the other feel bad for the way they naturally are. Insensitive comments are not helpful.

I have also noticed the 'Mr. Me Too' being a common theme. Some men will use what you tell them against you and pretend to be the man they think you need. They will agree with what you say and act like the man that you need in order to get what they want.

Jason went as far as writing out a list of how he wanted our relationship to be. He even took me ring shopping and told his family members about me. It was so convincing, but all in vain. **Be careful what you share, who you share with and when you share – if at all.** Leave some mystery to yourself and flow as the Lord leads.

As always, learning is a blessing, and this is why God gives us life. In my early teens, I was in unhealthy relationships and friendships where I was surrounded by people who smoked weed and drank a lot. I too indulged in these acts.

I did not know who I was, and the relationship was founded on coming together to please our flesh, particularly in eating out, having sex and enjoying each other's company.

I kept other men on the side too, in case the other relationships did not work out. I lied to myself that they were male friends when it was obvious that they liked me. Guess what? It was all a mess. I am so thankful that I did not marry any of my exes.

I would have been extremely miserable and do not think I would have written this book if I had stayed with any of my exes. I can see through my own experiences and have learnt to understand why it is important to wait on the Lord for my husband.

For years, I would deal with negative emotions from toxic relationships, getting high and wasting time. It was about time for me to move on when I re-dedicated my life back to Christ in 2013 and asked Him to take my heart for real.

Of course, Jesus was and is still here for me. He used His Word to heal, comfort and give me truth. *I realised that none of these men ever loved me*. They only got with me for convenience, so I accepted the truth. Thank you, Lord. Praise His Holy name!

A lot of relationships in society are not based on a strong, solid foundation. Some relationships do work out well because they are based on the solid rock of Christ Jesus, involving consistent work on both sides, prayer and sacrifice.

Others choose to live together before marriage, as they feel it is better financially than to wait after marriage. This is an issue, particularly amongst Christians and can definitely complicate things. To me, it makes a man less motivated to go for marriage, if he already getting husband benefits before the fact.

It seems that we are living in a generation that shies away from hard work. A microwave relationship will not go far, but hard work will withstand the storms.

As human beings, we can be risk being very quick to rush into marriage without praying and discerning. Divorce rates are high, even amongst believers. Waiting on the Lord is hard. I know, because I am doing it. But I would rather be obedient and walk in the lane God has destined me to be in, than enjoy temporary pleasure and suffer the consequences of a broken relationship simply due to my impatience.

I am six years in relationship with the Lord, and I am still unmarried. But I see things differently now. I know who I am and have developed self-confidence and self-love. I am walking in my purpose and have a deeper relationship with Jesus.

Being single has its ups and downs, but I am thankful for this season that I will not get back once married. Being an introvert really helps, too! This is because introverts thrive from their own company. God knows what He is doing, so trust Him. I pray you have personal revelation in this area too, if not already.

CHAPTER 10

SEX BEFORE MARRIAGE

If I could turn back the hands of time, I would prefer to be a virgin! All the heartache, soul ties, confusion and time wasted could have been saved. I probably would have an even stronger relationship with the Lord and would be using my story to encourage other people to do the same.

Nonetheless, in all things, I give thanks to God and move forward, because I am fully convinced that God has a greater plan for my life.

Isaiah 43:18-20 (NJKV) says, **"Do not remember the former things, nor consider the things of old. (19) Behold, I will do a new thing, now it shall spring forth; shall you not know it? I will even make a road in the wilderness and rivers in the desert. (20) The beast of the field will honour Me, the jackals and the ostriches, because I give waters in the wilderness and rivers in the desert, to give drink to My people, My chosen."**

The enemy always has plans to pervert the things of God, and this is something I always fight against, especially in prayer and fasting.

When Adam and Eve were created in Genesis, they were husband and wife. God started His story on earth with marriage, or a union.

Throughout the Bible, God describes His relationship with us as a union. This can also be compared to a husband and wife being together as a married unit. *Isaiah 54:5* talks about how Jesus calls the Church His bride, and when He will be coming back for His church in *Ephesians 5:25-27*. This is a running theme throughout the Bible. God has a deep, unexplainable and unending love for us, which is intimate and true.

Many people manipulate the word of God to justify their sin or cover up what they have done. This should not be so. Being humble, honest and truthful are signs of a good character, not blaming it on someone else, but taking responsibility. Thank God for His grace and mercy.

Some could argue and say there is no such thing as signing documents to legally bind a marriage, but in the Bible, couples that made a decision to come together sealed their marriage through intimacy. Examples include Abraham and Sarah, Hannah and Elkanah, Jacob and Rebecca, to name a few.

While this is true, I have other questions for you:
- Is car insurance in the Bible?
- Is a university degree certificate or driving licence in the Bible?
- What about a National Insurance Number or a Passport?

If you know the above are not in the Bible, why do you comply with them?

Romans 13:1-2 (NKJV) says: **"Let every soul be subject to the governing authorities. For there is no authority except from God, and the authorities that exist are appointed by God. (2) Therefore whoever resists the authority resists the ordinance of God, and those who resist will bring judgment on themselves."**

This scripture can be taken out of context. We live in a world where good is evil, and evil is good. Preachers and evangelists are being arrested for preaching the Gospel on the streets. The Good News of the Gospel is now being branded as a hate speech. Can you believe it?! We are really living in the last days.

The Bible calls us to spread the word of God to all nations, but somehow, we are being restricted due to what other people will think of us. On the other hand, some people believe that according to Romans 13:1-2, we must follow the law regardless of the outcome. Yes, it tells us to follow the law of the land. However, in this antichrist world, many laws can be set up against Biblical beliefs. So we **must** be led by the Holy Spirit in all things, knowing that He will back us all the way.

In certain areas of the United Kingdom, giving money to a homeless person can be seen as a bad thing because they could use it on drugs or alcohol. But what if the Holy Spirit leads you to do it?

By law, in order to get married in the Western region, documents would need to be signed and dated. However, contrary to popular beliefs, marriage is **more** than *just* a piece of paper. It is from God – His original design and plan. Due to the temptation of sexual immorality, it is better to get married, as it helps plan a solid foundation for a man and a woman to live out their God-given destiny with the right spouse. In particular, it builds a solid foundation for children to be born into and raised in the way of the Lord so they will not depart from it, in reference to Proverbs 22:6.

1 Corinthians 7:1-2 reads: **"Now concerning the things of which you wrote to me: It is good for a man not to touch a woman. (2) Nevertheless, because of sexual immorality, let each man have his own wife, and let each woman have her own husband."**

I like the way the Apostle Paul says it is good for a man **not to touch a woman.** People have tried to make me feel strange for having strict rules about touching prior to marriage, even when I was in a committed relationship.

My thoughts about this stand firm: kissing should not take place until marriage, particularly for those that are weaker in this area. Kissing on the cheek can suffice, but when you indulge with French kissing, it slowly prepares the body for sex.

Why start something you cannot finish and open the door for the enemy to tempt you? This can be a very sensitive topic, but it is important to lay the foundation right to ensure courting leads to a successful and healthy marriage.

Some may disagree and argue that it works for them. My point is you have to really know yourself rather than taking on the opinions of others.

With Kwame, I experienced a very short relationship in which we held hands, hugged sometimes, and from time to time, he kissed me on the cheek. Although it took me a few months to get over the relationship and heal from losing someone I thought I would marry, it was easier because we did not indulge in sex.

When you have experienced the bondage of sexual sin, you will understand why it is best to wait on the Lord. I had a former female prayer partner that expressed her high curiosity in sex.

She was a virgin, and I tried to tell her that she was not missing out on anything – that rushing into sex will lead to disappointment and heartbreak. If a man is willing to put you in a vulnerable situation of sexual sin, that is not love, but selfishness.

After all the relationships I have been through, I now know what I DESERVE! I understand my worth and will not be having sex until I am married! A real man of God that is truly interested in you as his wife will be mature enough to understand that sex *is* for marriage.

Of course, there will be temptation on both sides, but when we as children of God understand why sex is created, we will honour God with our bodies and be obedient to His Word. Revelation is key.

Sex creates a strong bond between two people that was only created to be enjoyed in the context of marriage. It is only safe in marriage when you are with your spouse, who God has confirmed is for you.

I believe in having a personal and active relationship with the Lord. This should be through prayer, Bible study and fasting on a regular basis. **God speaks to us in many different ways**. A running theme in my failed relationships is me not having peace about them. This made me start from ground level zero and work my way up to be at a healthy place in my relationship with God.

Galatians 5:22-23 (NKJV) says: **"(22) But the fruit of the Spirit is Love, Joy, Peace, Longsuffering, Kindness, Goodness, Faithfulness, (23) Gentleness, and Self-control. Against such there is no law."**

The fruits of the Spirit will enable one to be careful of going against what God has stated in His Word. If you want your husband or wife to cultivate all the fruits, then you also need to cultivate yours as well.

Some people may say: "We are engaged anyway, so why shouldn't we have sex?," or, "I can't find a man that will be celibate with me," or "He loves me," etc. If we are really honest with ourselves, there are adverse effects that come with fornication. The soul ties will be difficult to break. That is why keeping your body for one person is more beneficial.

Here are a few practical reasons why sex before marriage isn't ideal:

- Emotional ties to someone that is not your wife/husband can lead to disaster.
- Sex before marriage is distracting and does not consider God's Word or please Him in any way.
- The opposite sex tugging on your spirit to stay with them because they are 'lonely' can keep you in bondage longer.
- Participating in sex can give you the impression that you are already in too deep to leave.
- Unwanted/unplanned pregnancy – could potentially lead to an abortion for fear of family or friends finding out, and/or single parenthood is more likely.
- A number of Sexually Transmitted Diseases (STD's).

- Lack of motivation in waiting for God's best will be strengthened.
- Someone can get bored, and you will run the risk of being dumped.
- Respect for one another can be lost along the way due to the lack of respect for one another's body, the way God intended.
- Soul ties and delays in the spiritual realm are increased, as one would have to get over the other person, and the time can vary.
- This could lead to a lack of motivation to focus on work on oneself (i.e. counselling, mental health, building back a quality relationship with God).

Sex is safe in marriage as this was the way God intended it to be. There are people out there who believe this and will treat you with respect.

Looking back, I felt so terrible when disobeying God and fornicating. The Bible speaks of Adam and Eve being **naked and unashamed** in front of one another.

Waiting to have sex until marriage is God's plan, and it is a beautiful thing. *Genesis 2:24-25 (NKJV)* says: **"(24) Therefore a man shall leave his father and mother and be joined to his wife, and they shall become one flesh. (25) And they were both naked, the man and his wife, and were not ashamed."**

I believe one of the biggest mistakes we can make is marrying the wrong person. If we are blinded by sex and are weak emotionally, we can run the risk of creating heaps of baggage in our lives. Staying celibate and getting to know the person without being physical is rewarding.

If you remain celibate, you and your boyfriend or fiancé will discuss what you both want and build a friendship with a strong foundation that is Jesus Christ. God will never tempt you to have sex before marriage; His ways are not our ways.

In addition to this, words are powerful. Kwame told me, *"I cannot wait to marry you"* but ended up breaking up with me. It is emotionally draining to tell someone intimate and private things about who you are, only for the relationship to end. So, wait on the Lord.

Remember – we are called to be holy, which means to be set apart. We are called to be like Jesus. Let us focus on the right thing and allow the Holy Spirit to burn within us.

A question to consider is: How will *not* keeping my body pure draw me closer to God, allowing His will to be done in my life? Yes, God has given us free will to do what we please, but we must also consider the consequences of being out of His will. For further study, read **1 Corinthians 6:12-20.**

MY FINAL THOUGHTS

In all that I have been through, I am thankful for those within the body of Christ that have been there for me. I was introduced to my friend's Pastors because at the time I was going to a big church and did not feel comfortable opening up to the Pastors there about my personal issues because I did not know them well, nor did I feel led to approach them.

When I was engaged to my ex fiancé, he informed me that every man cheats, so I should settle in to being his second wife. False. My friend at the time told me that it was a pure lie, and I should not get back with him. I still believe there is a man for me that God is preparing. He is an Ephesians 5 man of God!

I believe the same for you, that whatever family situation you have faced in the past or at present, God will turn it around for your good and grant your heart's desires (in line with His will).

From a real and personal place, I have not seen the best examples in my own family, but I walk in what God has for me: I am living in the generation of Jesus and no longer believe in generational curses.

I would encourage you to maintain your high standards and keep your emotions in check by maintaining closeness with God. With standards (that are reasonable, of course!), you will easily be able to discern whether you should even speak to a man on a 'getting to know you' level.

For example, I recently gave my number to a man who approached me. I rarely do this. He was pleasant and presented as genuine. We spoke for a few weeks, but I noticed inconsistencies. It seemed that by the lack of communication he showed me, he was just not that into me.

I accepted that, God made our paths cross because we both had a word for one another. He encouraged me in an area that God was speaking to me at that particular time, and for that, I was thankful. So instead of me getting upset or clingy towards a man just because he was presented in front of me, I decided to apply wisdom.

In saying this, no one should be labelled as an option – God created us as more than that. Ladies, see things for what they are. If he is showing you signs that he is not into you, accept it. Close your legs and open your eyes. If he wants you, he will definitely let you know! One of the scriptures that I love, is **Proverbs 3:6: "In all your ways acknowledge Him, And He shall direct your paths."**

Work on yourself. In my six years of being single, this is one of the things that I have truly done. To name a few things, I have completed two degrees, started my business and continue to expand it, started exercising on a consistent basis, developed a healthier way of eating, saved my money, invested in myself, got to know myself through the word of God, and stopped taking drugs and drinking alcohol.

I worked on my image by bettering my wardrobe and seeking advice from a personal stylist, made better choices in the friends I make, looked deeper in myself and asked God to reveal the things that I need to work on personality-wise and heal from, sought out counselling, set high standards, and for the most part, kept my legs closed.

Above all, I have grown in my relationship with Jesus through my prayer life and understanding of His Word. The Word of God truly works, so apply it to your life! You are a wife, so live as one. You are worth the wait for sex, so just believe it! And even after you get married, never stop working on yourself.

Do not settle! When I meet someone, I have to remind myself of this. After being single for so long, do not just get with the first man that approaches you, or even the second or third!

Let God confirm. I understand that it can feel like there are not many great men out there or that your standards are too unrealistic. False. Sometimes people think that the whole courting/dating (however you describe as getting to know a man in Christ, with no sex) process is long, so sticking with a man that you know is not God's best for you seems more convenient.

But we Kingdom Women do not settle for scraps! Nor do we beg for anything. We are royalty, and we know it. Trust and believe that God has not forgotten about you. I said it before: God has already provided. When I encourage you to let God write your love story. Let it all play out. Trust Him that He has kept you and provided for your every need ***all this time.***

Speak life. Claim positivity. Just because your family may not have the best examples of relationships, that does not mean that you cannot be the first to birth a generation of successful relationships. Recently, I decided to claim that my situation has changed. Instead of moaning about how I have struggled in relationships all my life, I decided to speak life over my next one. We sometimes forget that life and death are in the power of the tongue (Proverbs 18:21). Therefore, speak well of yourself, and you will see things change for the better.

Try and find a way to understand the nature of a man. I accepted that men are different from women. It is important for me to know that men will not think the same way as me, nor should I expect them to. Men are naturally more logical, while women are more emotional, which makes them able to engage in sexual relationships and not get attached, like women often do.

We women find it easier to express our feelings, but this does not always come as naturally to men. I think men are pretty straightforward and you simply need to observe men and seek wise counsel. This will assist with knowledge and understanding regarding entering a relationship with a man to eventually marry him.

However, be careful not to label all men as the same because of bad experiences! Men are not the enemy, but the wrong one for you can be. Each man has his own personality, but the basic behaviours are generally common among men.

If a man is interested, you will not have to question it. I have noticed that this is a difficult concept for some women to understand. If you have to question it, then he is probably just not that into you! If he does not speak to you that much, is not interested in seeing you much, is talking about going on a break in your relationship or states that he is not ready for marriage, then he probably wants to see what else is out there because he is not 'sold' on you.

If he is showing you any signs that he is not that interested and is being inconsistent, then do not play yourself by waiting around. If he makes you feel bad about being celibate and is trying to push the boundaries by phoning you late or constantly talking to you about sex, perhaps you should just ignore him. It is ok if he is not for you. Keep it moving and do not beg or settle!

Do not give wife treatment to someone that is not your husband! I fell into this category in the past, cooking for a man and giving him my body. I am thankful that I did not actually live with these men, as I would have wasted more time. If you are in a relationship, just enjoy the season you are in. You have your whole life to be a wife to him so, just take it easy and do not get ahead of yourself.

Think twice before getting back with your ex. Remember why you broke up – the reason that the relationship did not work. People change, yes, but if he really was not able to be his best self when you were together, you probably were not the one for him anyway. A man that perceives his wife does all that he can to be his best for her. He will not break up with her or be neglectful.

Even if he knows you are the one and takes advantage of you, he will go **out of his way** to show you that he has changed. So, what if he is telling you he is now missing you because he sees that you are looking good and doing well on social media, but he showed no love in the relationship? He probably wants to get back with you to prove to his ego that he can. If you did not have sex with him in the past, he may want to see if he can get it this time around. Do not entertain nonsense! You really do not have to reply.

Get a mentor. When I left Jack initially, I remember being unable to stop crying. Looking back, I see the goodness of God when He used a Facebook friend that was located all the way in Nigeria, that I had never met, to counsel me via Skype calls and text messages. He listened to me, let me cry and express my feelings. He was basically a virtual mentor that gave me the raw truth that Jack really did not love me. I am so thankful, and I have learnt that God will **provide,** whenever and however!

Learn to respect a man. I have seen that disrespecting a man can shake up a relationship/marriage really badly. So practice respect with the males in your life now. There is a reason that the Bible instructs us to do so. By nature, a man being disrespected can lead him to be abusive. Do not try to find out! (Ephesians 5:33).

Learn what love is. Then you will be able to easily identify when you have met someone who loves you. **1 Corinthians 13:4-8** says: **"(4) Love suffers long and is kind; love does not envy; love does not parade itself, is not puffed up; (5) does not behave rudely, does not seek its own, is not provoked, thinks no evil; (6) does not rejoice in iniquity, but rejoices in the truth; (7) bears all things, believes all things, hopes all things, endures all things."** Study this.

In 1 Kings 11:4, we see generational curses through David and his son Solomon due to the number of wives and concubines they had, as well as being distracted and disobedient against the Will of God. It is a real thing, but the good news is that in Christ, we are set free. *John 8:36 (NKJV)* says: **"Therefore if the Son makes you free, you shall be free indeed."** Believe it and receive it.

Declare this: **My situation has changed. My past may have not gone as well as I wanted, but I now have Jesus. Thank you, Lord, for my future husband. Please guide me and help me to be ready for him. In Jesus' name, Amen!**

Never be afraid to ask, "Lord, is this relationship for me?" You have nothing to lose, and if you ask the Lord, He will tell you. God loves you and wants the best for you. He is a gentleman and will not force you, but He has His best for you.

If you feel that you need further support in the area of relationships and would like to work with me one-on-one, please email me at rosemarygodwinese@gmail.com for life and relationship coaching.

REFERENCES

- Pinky Promise Ministry:
  https://www.pinkypromisemovement.com/
- The Singleton by Christina Tosin Fasoro (can be found on Amazon)
- Breaking Soul Ties by Dephne Madyara (can be found on Amazon)
- Institute for Family Studies: Premarital Cohabitation Is Still Associated With Greater Odds of Divorce https://ifstudies.org/blog/premarital-cohabitation-is-still-associated-with-greater-odds-of-divorce

www.ingramcontent.com/pod-product-compliance
Lightning Source LLC
LaVergne TN
LVHW051645080426
835511LV00016B/2504